Also by the same author, and available in Coronet Books:

You're a Winner, Charlie Brown (1)
Good Ol' Snoopy (3)
Who do you think you are, Charlie Brown (4)
Fun with Peanuts (5)
You're my Hero, Charlie Brown (7)
This is Your Life, Charlie Brown (8)
All This and Snoopy, Too (11)
Good Grief, Charlie Brown! (12)
Here's To You, Charlie Brown (13)
Nobody's Perfect, Charlie Brown (14)
Very Funny, Charlie Brown (15)
Hey, Peanuts (17)
You're a Brave Man, Charlie Brown (18)
We Love You, Snoopy (19)
Peanuts for Everybody (20)
You're Too Much, Charlie Brown (21)
Here Comes Charlie Brown (22)
The Wonderful World of Peanuts (24)
What Next, Charlie Brown (26)
You're the Greatest, Charlie Brown (27)
It's For You, Snoopy (28)
Have It Your Way, Charlie Brown (29)
You're Not For Real, Snoopy (30)
You're Something Special, Snoopy (33)
Take It Easy, Charlie Brown (35)

You're a Pal, Snoopy!

Selected Cartoons from YOU NEED HELP, CHARLIE BROWN, Vol. 2

Charles M. Schulz

CORONET BOOKS
Hodder Fawcett, London

First published 1972 by Fawcett Publications Inc. New York

Coronet edition 1972
Second impression 1973
Third impression 1973
Fourth impression 1974
Fifth impression 1976

Printed and bound in Great Britain for Coronet Books, Hodder Fawcett, London, by Hazell Watson & Viney Ltd, Aylesbury, Bucks

ISBN 0 340 15696 1

MY HEART IS FULL ON THE DAY I FIRST GO OUT TO THE OL' BALL FIELD...
AH! THERE IT IS! MY PITCHER'S MOUND...COVERED WITH TRADITION..
I LOVE THE SMELL OF THE HORSEHIDE, THE GRASSY OUTFIELD AND THE DUSTY INFIELD...I LOVE THE MEMORIES..THE HOPES...AND THE DREAMS FOR THE NEW SEASON..
AND DANDELIONS!
SCHULZ

THIS PITCHER'S MOUND IS COVERED WITH DANDELIONS
DON'T TOUCH THEM, CHARLIE BROWN!
DON'T YOU DARE HURT ALL THOSE INNOCENT DANDELIONS! THEY'RE BEAUTIFUL! DON'T YOU DARE CUT THEM DOWN!
BESIDES, YOU MAY NOT KNOW IT, BUT YOU LOOK KIND OF CUTE STANDING THERE SURROUNDED BY DANDELIONS..
I DON'T WANT TO LOOK CUTE!!
SCHULZ

HERE WE GO... THE FIRST PITCH OF THE SEASON..
POW!
IT'S KIND OF PEACEFUL LYING HERE AMONG THE DANDELIONS..
SCHULZ

WHAT IN THE WORLD ARE ALL THESE DANDELIONS DOING ON THE PITCHER'S MOUND?
THEY GREW THERE! AND MY STUPID GIRL-OUTFIELDERS WON'T LET ME CUT THEM DOWN! THEY SAY THEY'RE PRETTY, AND I LOOK CUTE STANDING HERE AMONG THEM!
THEY'RE RIGHT...YOU DO LOOK KIND OF CUTE STANDING THERE..
SCHULZ

HOLD YOUR CHIN UP, CHARLIE BROWN..
I'M GOING TO TICKLE YOU WITH THIS DANDELION..IF YOUR CHIN TURNS YELLOW, IT MEANS YOU LIKE BUTTER..
?
HEY, LOOK! CHARLIE BROWN LIKES BUTTER!
I WONDER IF MY FONDNESS FOR DAIRY PRODUCTS WILL HELP US WIN BALL GAMES
SCHULZ

WHY, CHARLIE BROWN! YOU CUT DOWN ALL THE DANDELIONS!
YES, I CUT DOWN ALL THE DANDELIONS! THIS IS A PITCHER'S MOUND, NOT A FLOWER GARDEN!
SPEAKING OF FLOWER GARDENS, I'LL BET A CIRCLE OF DAFFODILS WOULD LOOK NICE AROUND THIS MOUND, DON'T YOU THINK SO?
OH, YES, VERY NICE...OR EVEN SOME MARIGOLDS..
I CAN'T STAND IT!
SCHULZ

WELL, WE LOST THE FIRST GAME OF THE SEASON AGAIN!
I SHOULDN'T LET IT BOTHER ME, BUT IT DOES...
WE ALWAYS SEEM TO LOSE THE FIRST GAME OF THE SEASON AND THE LAST GAME OF THE SEASON..
AND ALL THE STUPID GAMES IN-BETWEEN!
SCHULZ

THROW THIS GUY YOUR FAST BALL, CHARLIE BROWN..
I THINK YOU'D BETTER KEEP THE BALL LOW TO THIS GUY, CHARLIE BROWN...GIVE HIM A LOW CURVE..
THROW THIS GUY ALL KNUCKLE BALLS, CHARLIE BROWN...YOU'LL FOOL HIM WITH KNUCKLE BALLS...
THIS IS THE LATEST THING... PITCHING BY COMMITTEE!
SCHULZ

YOU GOT A "C" IN HISTORY? THAT'S ONLY AVERAGE!
SO WHAT? I'M AN AVERAGE STUDENT IN AN AVERAGE SCHOOL IN AN AVERAGE COMMUNITY....
WHAT'S WRONG WITH BEING AVERAGE?
BECAUSE YOU'RE CAPABLE OF DOING MUCH BETTER..
THAT'S THE AVERAGE ANSWER!
SCHULZ

YOU THINK BEING AVERAGE IS ENOUGH, DON'T YOU?
WELL, IT ISN'T!
WHAT SHAPE WOULD THE WORLD BE IN TODAY IF EVERYONE SETTLED FOR BEING AVERAGE?
WHAT SHAPE IS THE WORLD IN TODAY?
SCHULZ

IT'S JUST A LITTLE BRUISE... I THINK IT'LL BE ALL RIGHT...
SUPPERTIME? OH, YES...I THINK WE'LL BE FINISHED WELL BEFORE SUPPERTIME..
DO I THINK IT'S GOING TO RAIN? NO, I DOUBT IT...THOSE DON'T LOOK LIKE RAIN CLOUDS TO ME..
SOMETIMES I GET TO PITCH IN-BETWEEN QUESTIONS!
SCHULZ

PERHAPS I WAS A BIT TOO OBVIOUS!
SCHULZ

MISS OTHMAR?
SLURP SLURP

I WAS WONDERING IF YOU'D CARE TO RECONCILE OUR FAILURE TO SAY "GRACE" BEFORE DRINKING MILK WITH THE STORY OF DANIEL IN THE SIXTH CHAPTER OF THAT BOOK

OH...

MISS OTHMAR IS NEVER MUCH FOR RECONCILING...
SLURP
SLURP
SCHULZ

PTUI!
I MUST ADMIT I HAVE THE MOST UNIQUE DOUBLE-PLAY COMBINATION IN BASEBALL!
SCHULZ

I WONDER WHAT A DOG THINKS ABOUT WHEN HE SITS AND STARES LIKE THAT..
I CAN'T IMAGINE... THAT'S JUST ONE OF THOSE THINGS WE'LL NEVER KNOW...
SOMETIMES I MISS THE OL' PUPPY FARM!
SCHULZ

I WROTE A LETTER FOR SNOOPY TO THE DAISY HILL PUPPY FARM..
I HOPE THEY ANSWER RIGHT AWAY BECAUSE HE'S PRETTY EXCITED...HE WANTS TO TRY TO FIND HIS BROTHERS AND SISTERS...
I SUPPOSE HE'S WAITING RIGHT BY THE MAILBOX...
YES, I THINK YOU COULD SAY THAT..
SCHULZ

THIS LETTER IS FROM THE "DAISY HILL PUPPY FARM"
IT'S ADDRESSED TO YOU, SNOOPY, AND IT BEGINS, "DEAR SIR"
"DEAR SIR"?
THEY CALLED ME, "SIR"!
THEY CALLED ME, "SIR"! THEY CALLED ME, "SIR"! THEY CALLED ME, "SIR"!
WE'LL NEVER GET THIS LETTER READ
SCHULZ

..AND ONE BROTHER LIVES IN WASHINGTON, AND THE OTHER IN TEXAS..
ONE SISTER LIVES IN ST. LOUIS, ONE IN HOLLYWOOD AND ONE IN KANSAS...HOW ABOUT THAT?
WHY DON'T WE WRITE TO THEM, AND ARRANGE A FAMILY REUNION?
I THINK I'M GOING TO CRY...

SO YOU'RE GOING TO A FAMILY REUNION!
I'M VERY HAPPY FOR YOU, SNOOPY.. IT'LL BE FUN SEEING ALL YOUR BROTHERS AND SISTERS AGAIN...
OH! DON'T FORGET YOUR SUPPER DISH! EVERYONE WAS SUPPOSED TO BRING HIS OWN SUPPER DISH
SO LONG...HAVE A GOOD TIME!
SCHULZ

WELL, I SEE YOU'RE BACK!
HOW WAS THE FAMILY REUNION? DID YOU SEE ALL YOUR BROTHERS AND SISTERS? DID YOU HAVE A GOOD TIME? WHAT HAPPENED?
SIGH
THE ANTICIPATION FAR EXCEEDED THE ACTUAL EVENT!
SCHULZ

I HAD REALLY LOOKED FORWARD TO THAT FAMILY REUNION...
WHAT A DISAPPOINTMENT! NONE OF US SPOKE THE SAME LANGUAGE! WE WERE ALL STRANGERS
I NEVER SHOULD HAVE STARTED THAT WHOLE BUSINESS... IT WAS A BIG MISTAKE... I SHOULD HAVE KNOWN....
"YOU CAN'T GO HOME AGAIN"
SCHULZ

PSYCHIAT HELP 5¢
SO YOU WENT TO A FAMILY REUNION, AND YOU DIDN'T ENJOY IT...
THE DOCTOR IS IN
WELL, SO WHAT? DON'T FEEL GUILTY ABOUT IT! JUST BECAUSE YOU'RE RELATED TO PEOPLE DOESN'T MEAN YOU HAVE TO LIKE THEM!
THAT WILL BE FIVE CENTS, PLEASE
THE DOCTOR IS IN
I HATE IT WHEN I GET PAID IN DOG FOOD!
THE DOCTOR IS IN
SCHULZ

YOU'RE GETTING PRETTY GOOD ON THAT SKATEBOARD, LINUS!
BUT HE CAN'T DO "WHEELIES"!
SCHULZ

IT'S JUST NO USE! I CAN'T PRACTICE WITH YOU HANGING AROUND!
THE TRUTH IS YOU'RE EMBARRASSED BY A PRETTY FACE! THAT'S IT, ISN'T IT?
A PRETTY FACE MAKES YOU UNEASY, DOESN'T IT? HUH? DOESN'T IT?!
HE SHOULDN'T FEEL THAT WAY... LOTS OF PEOPLE GET EMBARRASSED IN THE PRESENCE OF A PRETTY FACE...
SCHULZ

YOU SAY YOU WANT ME TO BUNT? HOW DO YOU BUNT?
JUST HOLD THE BAT OUT IN FRONT OF YOU, AND TRY TO TAP THE BALL LIGHTLY...
I'M A GOOD MANAGER...IT'S ONLY THE MIDDLE OF MAY, AND ALREADY MY STOMACH HURTS!
SCHULZ

GUESS WHAT, SNOOPY...
I DID SOMETHING THAT WILL HELP MAKE YOUR FUR SHINY...
I MIXED A RAW EGG IN WITH YOUR DOG FOOD
I FEEL SICK!
SCHULZ

THERE ARE LEADERS IN THIS WORLD, CHARLIE BROWN, AND THERE ARE FOLLOWERS...
YOU ARE DOOMED ALWAYS TO BE A FOLLOWER! YOU WERE DOOMED FROM BIRTH...NOW, I HAVE A NEW THEORY....
IF YOU WERE TO OBSERVE CLOSELY, YOU'D NOTICE THAT FOR EVERY ELEVEN FOLLOWERS BORN INTO THIS WORLD, THERE IS ONE LEADER...
THAT'S MY NEW THEORY... BABIES ARE BORN IN SQUADS!
SCHULZ

I DIDN'T KNOW YOU HAD PLANTED FLOWERS AROUND SNOOPY'S DOGHOUSE
SURE, I DID IT WEEKS AGO... HE NEEDED A LITTLE COLOR AROUND THERE
DON'T YOU THINK IT WAS A GOOD IDEA?
WELL, I SUPPOSE SO...
BUT WHY SUNFLOWERS?
SCHULZ

I FEEL MEAN!
I HATE THE WHOLE WORLD!
BY GOLLY, NOBODY BETTER GET IN MY WAY TODAY!
I'M GONNA GET SLAUGHTERED, BUT I CAN'T RESIST THE CHALLENGE!
SCHULZ

FIGHT! FIGHT!
LUCY AND SNOOPY ARE HAVING A FIGHT!
!
GOOD GRIEF!
STAND STILL, AND FIGHT LIKE A MAN!!
SCHULZ

SWISH!
SLURP SLURP SLURP SLURP
SWISH!
SLURP! SLURP! SLURP!
WHAT IN THE WORLD KIND OF STUPID FIGHT IS THIS?!
SCHULZ

HERE, NOW! YOU TWO STOP THAT FIGHTING! STOP IT, I SAY!
SLURP! SLURP! SLURP!
WHO'S FIGHTING? I SURRENDER!
I SAID, I SURRENDER! STOP IT! I SURRENDER! I SURRENDER!
I SAID, I SURRENDER!!!
SCHULZ

I'M SURPRISED AT YOU TWO!
BRAWLING IN THE STREET LIKE A COUPLE OF HOODS! WHAT'S THE MATTER WITH YOU?!
HE WAS STANDING WHERE I WANTED TO WALK!
THE ULTIMATE CRIME!
SCHULZ

I HAVE MIXED EMOTIONS ABOUT THAT FIGHT..
I HATE BRAWLING, BUT I HAVE TO ADMIT THAT I ADMIRE THE WAY YOU STOOD UP TO LUCY
I'D E EN LIKE TO SHAKE YOUR HAND, BUT IM AFRAID SHE MIGHT SEE ME..
HOW WISHY-WASHY CAN YOU GET?
SCHULZ

AS SOON AS SCHOOL IS OVER, I HAVE TO GO TO CAMP FOR TWO WEEKS..
I DON'T REALLY CARE MUCH ABOUT GOING TO CAMP...I'M AFRAID I'LL GET LONESOME
I'M AFRAID THAT WHEN I'M MILES AWAY FROM HOME, I'LL START TO MISS MY FRIENDS
WHAT FRIENDS?
SCHULZ

IF YOU DON'T WANT TO GO TO CAMP, CHARLIE BROWN, WHY GO?
I FEEL OBLIGATED

MY MOM AND DAD THINK THEY'RE DOING ME A FAVOR... THEY'RE HAPPY BECAUSE THEY THINK THIS WILL BE A GOOD EXPERIENCE FOR ME

RATS!

POOR GOOD OL' CHARLIE BROWN...
SCHULZ

PSYCHIATRIC HELP 5¢
THIS FEAR OF GOING TO CAMP IS SOMETHING YOU'VE GOT TO OVERCOME!
THE DOCTOR IS IN
IT'LL BE GOOD FOR YOU! IT'LL TEACH YOU TO STAND ON YOUR OWN TWO FEET! THIS IS JUST THE SORT OF EXPERIENCE YOU NEED!
THE DOCTOR
HOW ABOUT YOU? ARE YOU GOING TO CAMP THIS SUMMER?
PSYCHIATRIC HELP 5¢
THE DOCTOR IS IN
AND LEAVE MY GOOD HOME? DON'T BE RIDICULOUS!!!
THE DOCTOR IS IN
SCHULZ

WELL, OLD FRIEND, I'M OFF TO CAMP FOR TWO WEEKS..
I JUST WANTED TO SAY "GOOD-BY" BEFORE I LEFT... I KNOW I'M GOING TO MISS YOU..
I SUPPOSE YOU'LL MISS ME, TOO, BUT I GUESS WE...
Z
SIGH
SCHULZ

WELL, HERE I AM ON A BUS GOING TO CAMP
THESE CAMP BUSES ARE PRETTY NICE, I GUESS...
SIGH WE'VE ONLY BEEN ON THIS BUS FOR TEN MINUTES, AND ALREADY I'M LONESOME..
I FEEL LIKE I'M BEING DRAFTED!
SCHULZ

WELL, HERE I AM AT CAMP STANDING IN MY FIRST CHOW LINE...LUNCH IS GONNA TASTE GOOD
WHAT'S YOUR NAME, KID?
CHARLIE BROWN
HEY, GET A LOAD OF THE KID WITH THE FUNNY NAME!
LUNCH IS GONNA TASTE AWFUL!
SCHULZ

DEAR MOM AND DAD,
HOW ARE YOU?
I AM FINE.
MY FIRST DAY OF CAMP IS OVER.
I LIVED THROUGH IT.
SCHULZ

A LETTER FROM LINUS! WELL, I'LL BE!
DEAR CHARLIE BROWN...HOW ARE YOU ENJOYING CAMP? I SUPPOSE YOU ARE WORRIED ABOUT YOUR BASEBALL TEAM..
WELL, DON'T WORRY...WE'RE DOING FINE...IN FACT, YESTERDAY WE WON THE FIRST GAME WE'VE WON ALL SEASON!
SIGH
SCHULZ

SNIF!
?
EXCUSE ME, BUT I COULDN'T HELP OVERHEARING YOU CRYING.. WHAT'S THE MATTER?
I DON'T KNOW... I GUESS I'M JUST LONESOME..
FRIEND!!
SCHULZ

ROY, YOU'VE GOT TO SNAP OUT OF IT!
A CAMP LIKE THIS IS THE BEST PLACE FOR SOMEONE LIKE YOU...IT HELPS YOU TO BREAK THOSE OLD APRON STRINGS!
LIFE IS FULL OF EXPERIENCES THAT HAVE TO BE FACED ALONE!
BUT YOU SAID YOU WERE LONESOME, TOO..
I TALK A GOOD CAMP...
SCHULZ

DEAR MOM AND DAD,
THINGS ARE GOING BETTER HERE AT CAMP.
Yesterday I met this kid named Charlie Brown.
HE WAS VERY LONESOME, BUT I THINK I HAVE HELPED HIM.
He's the kind who makes a good temporary friend.
SCHULZ

C'MON, ROY, WE'LL BE LATE FOR THE "SING OUT"
WE'RE ALL GOING TO SIT AROUND THE CAMPFIRE, AND SING SONGS...
MAYBE I SHOULDN'T GO...
THOSE WORLD WAR I SONGS ALWAYS GET ME RIGHT HERE

STRIKE THREE!
WHAT'S THE MATTER, KID? AIN'TCHA NEVER PLAYED BASEBALL BEFORE?!!
WHY DIDN'T YOU TELL HIM, CHARLIE BROWN? WHY DIDN'T YOU TELL HIM ABOUT HOW YOU'RE THE MANAGER OF A TEAM AT HOME?
SOMEHOW, MENTIONING A TEAM THAT HAS THREE GIRL-OUTFIELDERS AND A DOG-SHORTSTOP DIDN'T SEEM QUITE APPROPRIATE!
SCHULZ

WELL, SO LONG, CHARLIE BROWN... IT'S BEEN NICE KNOWING YOU..
IT'S BEEN NICE KNOWING YOU, TOO, ROY....HAVE A GOOD TRIP HOME..
FOR THE FIRST TIME IN MY LIFE I FEEL I REALLY HELPED SOMEONE...HE WAS LONESOME, AND I BECAME HIS FRIEND...
WHAT AN ACCOMPLISHMENT!
SCHULZ

WELL, HERE I AM ON THE BUS RETURNING HOME FROM CAMP
HERE'S THE STATION..I'M ALMOST HOME...I CAN'T BELIEVE IT...
LOOK! THERE'S SOME KIDS ALL LINED UP JUST GETTING READY TO LEAVE FOR CAMP...
LET 'EM GO! I'VE DONE MY HITCH!!
SCHULZ

OH, BOY! IS IT EVER GOOD TO BE BACK HOME!
HI, LUCY! I'M BACK!
YOU'RE WHAT?
I SAID, I'M BACK!
HAVE YOU BEEN AWAY?
SCHULZ

ALL RIGHT, SNOOPY, THIS IS THE LAST OF THE NINTH...WE NEED ONE RUN TO TIE UP THE GAME..
I WANT YOU TO GO UP THERE WITH TEETH-GRITTING DETERMINATION, AND GET ON BASE! LET'S SEE YOU GRIT YOUR TEETH...
THAT'S FINE...KEEP GRITTING YOUR TEETH, AND YOU'LL GET A HIT!
I FEEL LIKE A FOOL...
SCHULZ

LOOK AT THAT! LINUS GOT A HIT, TOO! I KNEW WE STILL HAD A CHANCE!
IF YOU GRIT YOUR TEETH, AND SHOW REAL DETERMINATION, YOU ALWAYS HAVE A CHANCE! YOU'RE UP NEXT, LUCY...LET'S SEE YOU GRIT YOUR TEETH...
FANTASTIC! YOU'LL SCARE THEIR PITCHER TO DEATH! KEEP GRITTING YOUR TEETH, AND GO GET A HIT!
GET A HIT?! I CAN'T EVEN SEE WHERE I'M GOING..
SCHULZ

STRIKE ONE!
OOOOOO! C'MON, CHARLIE BROWN, HIT IT! FOR ONCE IN YOUR LIFE, HIT IT!!
WOULDN'T YOU LIKE JUST FOR ONCE TO SEE CHARLIE BROWN HIT THAT BALL?
NO..
I'M NOT PREPARED TO HAVE THE WORLD COME TO AN END!
SCHULZ

STRIKE TWO!
NOW, I'M GOING TO GRIT MY TEETH, AND BEAR DOWN! IF A PERSON GRITS HIS TEETH, AND SHOWS REAL DETERMINATION, HE CAN'T FAIL!
STRIKE THREE!
YOU BLOCKHEAD!
SCHULZ

I STRUCK OUT, AND I LET MY TEAM DOWN...I'M NO GOOD FOR ANYTHING..
I'M JUST NO GOOD...I SHOULDN'T EVER TRY TO DO ANYTHING... I'M NO GOOD...I SHOULD JUST STAY IN BED FOR THE REST OF MY LIFE, AND SLEEP!
I CAN'T EVEN SLEEP GOOD!
SCHULZ

YOUR TROUBLE, CHARLIE BROWN, IS THAT YOU LIVE BY MOTTOS AND TRITE SAYINGS..
YOU REALLY THOUGHT THAT IF YOU GRITTED YOUR TEETH IT WOULD HELP YOU TO BECOME A HERO.. WELL, THERE'S MORE TO LIFE THAN JUST GRITTING YOUR TEETH...
CHARLIE BROWN, DO YOU UNDERSTAND WHAT I'M TRYING TO TELL YOU?
MAYBE I DIDN'T GRIT THEM HARD ENOUGH...MAYBE IF I...
SIGH!
SCHULZ

PERHAPS YOU SHOULDN'T BE A PLAYING MANAGER, CHARLIE BROWN..PERHAPS YOU SHOULD BE A BENCH MANAGER..
THAT'S A GOOD IDEA... YOU'D BE A GREAT BENCH MANAGER, CHARLIE BROWN...
YOU COULD SAY, "BENCH, DO THIS! BENCH, DO THAT!" YOU COULD EVEN BE IN CHARGE OF WHERE WE PUT THE BENCH..
WHEN THE TEAM GETS TO THE BALL PARK, YOU COULD SAY, "LET'S PUT THE BENCH HERE!" OR, "LET'S PUT THE BENCH THERE!"
I CAN'T STAND IT!
SCHULZ

THERE'S A RUMOR GOING AROUND THAT I WON'T BE PLAYING ANY MORE..
WELL, I'M NOT QUITTING BASEBALL JUST BECAUSE I GOOFED A FEW TIMES! I'M STILL THE MANAGER OF THIS TEAM, AND WHAT I SAY GOES!
NOW, THERE'S STILL TIME LEFT IN THIS SEASON FOR US TO MAKE A GOOD SHOWING IF WE'LL ALL JUST GRIT OUR TEETH, AND..
SCHULZ

GOOD NIGHT, SNOOPY..
DON'T STAY UP TOO LATE WATCHING TELEVISION
IT'S A GREAT TEMPTATION...
SCHULZ

YOU KNOW WHAT MAKES ME SICK? SEEING YOU DRAG THAT BLANKET AROUND!
IF OUR "BLANKET-HATING GRANDMA" WERE HERE, YOU WOULDN'T BE SO SMUG! SHE THINKS LETTING KIDS HAVE SECURITY BLANKETS IS STUPID
I AGREE WITH HER..I GUESS I MUST TAKE AFTER HER..
THAT'S ALWAYS BEEN THE TROUBLE WITH OUR FAMILY..WE HAVE TOO MUCH HEREDITY
SCHULZ

I HAVE A NEW AMBITION...
WHEN I GET BIG, I'D LIKE TO BE A BASEBALL UMPIRE..
WHAT IN THE WORLD MAKES YOU THINK YOU COULD BE A GOOD BASEBALL UMPIRE?
BECAUSE I'M ALWAYS RIGHT!
SCHULZ

SHOW-TIME AGAIN! SIGH
EVERY SATURDAY AFTERNOON I GO TO THE SHOW...IT'S SURPRISING HOW QUICKLY THE WEEKS GO BY WHEN YOU DO THE SAME THING EVERY SATURDAY
I SHOULD DO SOMETHING DIFFERENT
IT'S MAKING MY LIFE GO BY TOO FAST!
SCHULZ

AREN'T YOU GOING TO BE IN YOUR PSYCHIATRY BOOTH TODAY?
NO, BUT I HAVE A NEW ASSISTANT.. HE'LL BE GLAD TO HELP YOU...
PSYCHIATRIC HELP 5¢
THE DOCTOR IS REAL IN
I'M VERY DEPRESSED.. LIFE SEEMS TO HAVE LOST ALL MEANING...
GO HOME AND LISTEN TO A BRAHMS PIANO QUARTET... FIVE CENTS, PLEASE!
JUST HOW CAREFULLY DO YOU SCREEN THESE ASSISTANTS OF YOURS?
SCHULZ

HEY, MANAGER, WAIT! I HAVE A QUESTION..
I'VE BEEN READING ABOUT THIS BASEBALL STADIUM THAT HAS PLASTIC GRASS...HOW COME WE DON'T HAVE PLASTIC GRASS?
STANDING OUT HERE IN THE OUTFIELD LIKE THIS, LOTS OF QUESTIONS COME TO YOUR MIND
SCHULZ

I'VE GOT TO SHOW THAT BEACH-BEAGLE WHAT A GREAT SURFER I AM!
I'LL PROVE TO HER I'M NO HODAD... I'LL IMPRESS HER WITH SOME FAST TURNS AND HOTDOGGING..
COWABUNGA!
ISN'T THAT YOUR DOG OUT THERE, CHARLIE BROWN? I THINK HE'S LOST HIS MIND!
SCHULZ

LOOK AT THAT CRAZY DOG...HE'S GOING TO....
WIPE OUT!
GOOD GRIEF!
SCHULZ

WELL, WE LOST AGAIN, BUT WHO CARES?
SURE, IT'S ONLY A GAME...WE LOST, BUT SO WHAT? WHO CARES?
JUST WHAT I'VE ALWAYS BEEN AFRAID OF... MY TEAM HAS BUILT UP AN IMMUNITY TO LOSING!
SCHULZ

I LIKE BEETHOVEN, BUT BRAHMS MAKES ME GLAD I'M ALIVE..
I THINK I'LL GO HOME, AND LISTEN TO BRAHMS' FOURTH...
I FEEL THE NEED TO HAVE THE FEELING THAT IT'S GOOD TO BE ALIVE..
I KNOW WHAT YOU MEAN...
THAT'S A TERRIBLE FEELING TO HAVE THE NEED OF HAVING THE FEELING OF HAVING...
SCHULZ

YOU'RE NOT HAPPY, ARE YOU?
SCHULZ

YOU'RE THINKING OF KICKING OVER MY SAND CASTLE, AREN'T YOU?
WELL, WAIT JUST A MOMENT, WILL YOU, PLEASE, WHILE I STAND UP?
THIS WILL GIVE ME A CHANCE TO..
BEAT YOU TO IT!!!
SCHULZ

PIG-PEN, YOU ARE A PERPETUAL MESS...
I CAN TELL JUST WHERE YOU'VE BEEN ALL WEEK FROM THE DIRT ON YOUR CLOTHES...YESTERDAY YOU WERE DOWN BY THE TRAIN TRACKS..
YOU SPENT THE DAY BEFORE DOWN AT THE PLAYGROUND, THE DUMP AND THE WAREHOUSE..
I DON'T HAVE TO LISTEN TO THIS..
AND MONDAY YOU SPENT ALL DAY AT THE BRICK YARD, ISN'T THAT RIGHT?
SCHULZ

I'M GOING TO TRY FOR A HOME RUN, CHARLIE BROWN!
EITHER WE WIN OR WE LOSE! ALL OR NOTHING!
THAT'S THE SPIRIT! GO FOR BROKE!
SYDNEY OR THE BUSH!
"SYDNEY OR THE BUSH"?
SCHULZ

I HAVE NEVER SEEN THE SKY AS BLUE AS IT IS TODAY..
OH, I HAVE... I REMEMBER BACK ON JULY 14, 1959, THE SKY WAS REAL BLUE...OH, YES, IT WAS MUCH BLUER THAT DAY...
AND THEN I ALSO REMEMBER ON SEPTEMBER 2, 1961, THE SKY WAS A VERY DEEP BLUE...
AND ON JUNE 1ST OF THE VERY NEXT YEAR THE SKY WAS..
I CAN'T STAND IT...
SCHULZ

WHY AREN'T YOU A PONY?!!
SCHULZ

CHARLIE BROWN, THERE'S A BOY OUTSIDE WHO PUSHED ME DOWN...
I TOLD HIM I'D GET MY BIG BROTHER AFTER HIM SO I WANT YOU TO GO OUT THERE, AND SLUG HIM
YOU MEAN YOU WANT ME TO GO OUTSIDE, AND FIND OUT WHAT HIS PURPOSE WAS IN PUSHING YOU DOWN, AND ASK HIM NOT TO DO IT AGAIN..
NO, I WANT YOU TO GO OUT THERE, AND **SLUG** HIM!
THAT'S WHAT I WAS AFRAID OF...
SCHULZ

THAT BOY OUTSIDE PUSHED ME DOWN, AND YOU'RE AFRAID TO DO SOMETHING ABOUT IT! A FINE BROTHER YOU ARE!
ALL RIGHT! I'LL GO OUT THERE! I'LL EITHER TEACH HIM A LESSON, OR GET MYSELF KILLED!
THAT'S THE SPIRIT!! "SYDNEY OR THE BUSH"!
"SYDNEY OR THE BUSH"?
SCHULZ

WHY DID YOU WRITE, "CHARLIE BROWN IS A BLOCKHEAD" ON THE SIDEWALK?
BECAUSE I SINCERELY BELIEVE YOU ARE A BLOCKHEAD! I HAVE TO WRITE WHAT I BELIEVE IS TRUE.. IT'S MY MORAL RESPONSIBILITY!
DEEP DOWN I ADMIRE HER INTEGRITY..
SCHULZ

I SUPPOSE I REALLY SHOULD TELL SOMEBODY..
BUT THEN AGAIN, WHY SHOULD I? IT'S MY SECRET...WHY SHOULDN'T I KEEP IT TO MYSELF?
IT'S KIND OF NICE HAVING A SECRET...
I'M THE ONLY PERSON WHO KNOWS THAT THERE ARE DOGS ON THE MOON!
SCHULZ

IT'S A GOOD THUMB, BUT NOT A GREAT THUMB!
SCHULZ

SCHROEDER, DO YOU THINK I'M BEAUTIFUL?
I THINK YOU'RE THE MOST BEAUTIFUL GIRL THE WORLD HAS EVER KNOWN...
YOU HATE ME, DON'T YOU?
SCHULZ

LISTEN TO THIS..
IT SAYS HERE THAT BY 1980 THERE WILL BE A NEED FOR 47,250 VETERINARIANS...
BUT IT ALSO SAYS THAT THERE WILL BE A SHORTAGE OF OVER 8000 VETERINARIANS...
REMIND ME NOT TO BE SICK IN 1980!
SCHULZ

WHAT'S THIS?
I HAVE HEARD THAT IT IS BETTER TO LIGHT A SINGLE CANDLE THAN TO CURSE THE DARKNESS
THAT'S TRUE..ALTHOUGH THERE WILL ALWAYS BE THOSE WHO WILL DISAGREE WITH YOU....
YOU STUPID DARKNESS!
SCHULZ

DEAR PENCIL-PAL,
HAVE YOU HAD A NICE SUMMER?
I LIKE TO READ, DO YOU? I AM VERY FOND OF BOOKS.
I CAN ALWAYS ENJOY A GOOD BOOK. I HAVE ALWAYS BEEN THE SORT OF PERSON WHO ENJOYS READING.
WHEN I HAVE NOTHING ELSE TO DO, I READ.
SCHULZ

HOMEWORK ALREADY! WRITE A THOUSAND-WORD ESSAY ON WHAT WE DID DURING THE SUMMER!
NOBODY CAN WRITE A THOUSAND-WORD ESSAY ON WHAT HE DID DURING THE SUMMER! IT'S RIDICULOUS!
WHEN ARE YOU GOING TO TRY TO WRITE YOURS... THIS EVENING?
MINE'S ALREADY FINISHED..I WROTE IT DURING STUDY PERIOD!
YOU DRIVE ME CRAZY!!!
SCHULZ

DO YOU KNOW WHY ENGLISH TEACHERS GO TO COLLEGE FOR FOUR YEARS?
NO, I DON'T KNOW WHY ENGLISH TEACHERS GO TO COLLEGE FOR FOUR YEARS..
WELL, THEN I'LL TELL YOU WHY ENGLISH TEACHERS GO TO COLLEGE FOR FOUR YEARS....
SO THEY CAN MAKE STUPID LITTLE KIDS WRITE STUPID ESSAYS ON WHAT THEY DID ALL STUPID SUMMER!!
SCHULZ

English Essay
"What I Did This Summer"
I played ball, and
I went to camp.
ONE, TWO, THREE, FOUR, FIVE, SIX, SEVEN, EIGHT....
NINE HUNDRED AND NINETY-TWO WORDS TO GO!
SCHULZ

YOU'RE CUTE, YOU KNOW THAT?
YOU'RE SO CUTE I THINK I'M GOING TO GIVE YOU A BIG HUG AND A KISS ON THE NOSE!
THAT'S REAL CONCENTRATION
SCHULZ

I WONDER IF THERE ARE "PEOPLE" STARS AND "DOG" STARS ?
SCHULZ

BLEAH!
BLEAH!
BLEAH!
BLEAH!
AAUGH! OUR TONGUES TOUCHED! MY TONGUE TOUCHED THE TONGUE OF A DOG! I'M POISONED!
BLEAH!
I FEEL A LITTLE NAUSEATED MYSELF!
SCHULZ

AND THEN HE WROTE THE GREAT NINTH SYMPHONY..
PSYCHIATRIC HELP 5¢
THE DOCTOR IS IN
BUT HE WAS DEAF! HE NEVER HAD A CHANCE TO HEAR IT PERFORMED! ISN'T THAT TERRIBLE? THAT REALLY DEPRESSES ME...
TRY NOT TO THINK ABOUT IT.... FIVE CENTS, PLEASE!
THE DOCTOR IS IN
SOME CASES ARE RELATIVELY SIMPLE
THE DOCTOR IS IN
SCHULZ

PSYCHIATRI HELP 5¢
EVERYTHING SEEMS HOPELESS...
THE DOCTOR IS IN
I'M COMPLETELY DEPRESSED..
THE DOCTOR IS IN
GO HOME, AND EAT A JELLY-BREAD SANDWICH FOLDED OVER...FIVE CENTS, PLEASE
THE DOCTOR IS IN
THERE ARE SOME CURES YOU DON'T LEARN IN MEDICAL SCHOOL
THE DOCTOR IS IN
SCHULZ

RATS!
DO YOU SEE THIS FINGER? I CUT IT OPENING A STUPID CAN OF DOG FOOD FOR YOUR STUPID SUPPER! I HOPE YOU APPRECIATE IT!
HOW CAN I EAT WHEN I FEEL GUILTY?
SCHULZ

WHY DO THESE THINGS ALWAYS HAVE TO HAPPEN TO ME?
MY FINGER, WHICH I CUT OPENING A CAN OF DOG FOOD FOR YOUR SUPPER, HURT ALL LAST NIGHT! AGAIN I SAY, I HOPE YOU APPRECIATE IT!
BESIDES THAT, IT WASN'T A FINGER, IT WAS MY THUMB!
HE SHOULD COMPLAIN... I DON'T EVEN HAVE A THUMB!
SCHULZ

DO YOU REALIZE SNOOPY HASN'T EATEN HIS SUPPER IN TWO DAYS?
YOU MEAN BECAUSE OF MY CUT THUMB?
YES, BECAUSE OF YOUR STUPID CUT THUMB! HE FEELS RESPONSIBLE..
AND ON TOP OF IT, HE REFUSES TO EAT UNTIL YOUR THUMB IS COMPLETELY HEALED!
I AM A MARTYR!
OH, GOOD GRIEF!
SCHULZ

PSYCHIATRIC HELP 5¢
I'M WORRIED ABOUT MY DAD...
THE DOCTOR IS
EVERY NIGHT HE SITS IN THE KITCHEN EATING COLD CEREAL AND LOOKING AT THE PICTURES IN HIS OLD HIGH SCHOOL YEAR BOOK
HOW OLD IS YOUR FATHER?
I THINK HE JUST TURNED FORTY...
THE DOCTOR IS
NOTHING TO WORRY ABOUT... HE'S RIGHT ON SCHEDULE! FIVE CENTS, PLEASE...
THE DOCTOR
SCHULZ

"SETS"..... "ONE TO ONE MATCHING"..
"EQUIVALENT SETS".... "NON-EQUIVALENT SETS".... "SETS OF ONE"..."SETS OF TWO"..
"RENAMING TWO"..."SUBSETS"... "JOINING SETS"..."NUMBER SENTENCES"..."PLACEHOLDERS"...
ALL I WANT TO KNOW IS, HOW MUCH IS TWO AND TWO?
SCHULZ

SALLY, I'VE ASKED LINUS TO COME OVER TO HELP YOU WITH THIS "NEW MATH"
I COULDN'T BE LESS INTERESTED! WHAT DO I CARE ABOUT "NEW MATH"? I'M ONLY GOING TO BE A HOUSEWIFE!
THAT'S THE WRONG ATTITUDE...MATH CAN BE A VERY REWARDING SUBJECT...
HA!
I NEVER KNOW HOW TO ANSWER THAT..
SCHULZ

KEEP IN MIND THAT A NUMERAL STANDS FOR A CERTAIN NUMBER OF OBJECTS...
NOW, WHEN YOU COUNT, WHAT YOU ARE DOING IS MATCHING ELEMENTS ONE-TO-ONE WITH A SET OF COUNTING NUMBERS...
IN A SET OF NUMBERS, THE LAST NUMERAL MATCHED TO THAT SET IS THE CARDINAL NUMBER..
THERE'S A GOOD PROGRAM ON TV TONIGHT AT SEVEN O'CLOCK
SCHULZ

TODAY I WANT TO TALK TO YOU ABOUT RENAMING NUMBERS OR "EQUATIONS"
THIS IS A CONCEPT WHICH WILL BE CARRIED OVER WHEN YOU BEGIN TO STUDY ALGEBRA..
ALGEBRA?
DON'T TALK TO ME ABOUT ALGEBRA! I DON'T EVEN UNDERSTAND MATH! YOU'LL DRIVE ME CRAZY!
I'M LOSING MY MIND, AND NOBODY CARES!!
SCHULZ

YOU KNOW WHAT, SNOOPY?
I'LL BET WHEN YOU WERE A LITTLE KID, YOU NEVER HAD TO WORRY ABOUT "NEW MATH" OR "OLD MATH" OR ANY KIND OF MATH
THAT'S TRUE..AT THE DAISY HILL PUPPY FARM THAT WASN'T VERY IMPORTANT...
WHEN ALL YOU HAVE TO COUNT ARE THE HOURS TO SUPPERTIME, IT DOESN'T MATTER WHETHER YOU USE "OLD MATH" OR "NEW MATH"!
SCHULZ

I will not talk in class.
I will not talk in class.
I will not talk in class.
I will not talk in class.
I will not talk in class.
I will not talk in class.
I will not talk in class.
I will not talk in class.
On the other hand, who knows what I'll do?
SCHULZ

I THINK I'LL GO OVER AND INTRODUCE MYSELF TO THAT LITTLE RED-HAIRED GIRL
I THINK I'LL INTRODUCE MYSELF, AND THEN ASK HER TO COME OVER AND SIT NEXT TO ME
I THINK I'LL ASK HER TO SIT NEXT TO ME HERE, AND THEN I THINK I'LL TELL HER HOW MUCH I'VE ALWAYS ADMIRED HER...
I THINK I'LL FLAP MY ARMS, AND FLY TO THE MOON
SCHULZ

ASK LUCY WHO TOOK THE LAST PIECE OF CAKE
TELL HIM WHAT HE DOESN'T KNOW WON'T HURT HIM...
WHAT YOU DO NOT KNOW WILL NOT DO YOU ANY PHYSICAL DAMAGE!
SCHULZ

AN ENVELOPE FOR ME...
U.S. MAIL
WELL! THIS IS A NICE ONE...
A BLANKET? HOW COME YOU'RE GETTING A BLANKET IN THE MAIL?
I JOINED THE "SECURITY-BLANKET-OF-THE-MONTH CLUB"
SCHULZ

I CAN'T BELIEVE IN "THE GREAT PUMPKIN" BECAUSE I'VE NEVER SEEN HIM!
BUT HE EXISTS, I TELL YOU! ON HALLOWEEN NIGHT HE RISES OUT OF THE PUMPKIN PATCH, AND FLIES THROUGH THE AIR!
I THINK YOU HAVE HIM CONFUSED WITH SANTA CLAUS
WOULD I CONFUSE THE SUN AND THE MOON?
WOULD I CONFUSE NBC WITH CBS? WOULD I CONFUSE THE AMERICAN LEAGUE WITH THE NATIONAL LEAGUE? WOULD I?
I CAN'T STAND IT..
SCHULZ

DEAR GREAT PUMPKIN, SOMETHING HAS OCCURRED TO ME.
YOU MUST GET DISCOURAGED BECAUSE MORE PEOPLE BELIEVE IN SANTA CLAUS THAN IN YOU.
WELL, LET'S FACE IT... SANTA CLAUS HAS HAD MORE PUBLICITY.
BUT BEING NUMBER TWO, PERHAPS YOU TRY HARDER.
SCHULZ

OH, HI! LINUS? JUST A MINUTE... I'LL GET HIM..
IT'S FOR YOU...IT'S CHARLIE BROWN..
I'M NOT SPEAKING TO HIM..HE INSULTED MY BELIEF!
I'M NOT SPEAKING TO ANYONE WHO DOESN'T BELIEVE IN THE "GREAT PUMPKIN"!
GOOD LUCK WITH THE WORLD!
SCHULZ

I'M DEPRESSED... LINUS IS MAD AT ME BECAUSE I DON'T BELIEVE IN THE "GREAT PUMPKIN"
DON'T BE TOO DEPRESSED, CHARLIE BROWN...BEETHOVEN ALSO HAD PROBLEMS...
WHAT'S THAT GOT TO DO WITH IT?
NOTHING, I GUESS.. IT JUST CAME TO MY MIND..
OH, GOOD GRIEF!
SCHULZ

WELL, HAS THE "GREAT PUMPKIN" COME YET?
WHAT DO YOU CARE, CHARLIE BROWN?
I'M SORRY I INSULTED YOUR BELIEF...I DON'T THINK ANY POINT OF DOCTRINE IS WORTH SPLITTING UP A FRIENDSHIP...I APOLOGIZE...
I APOLOGIZE, TOO, CHARLIE BROWN... SIT DOWN, AND WE'LL WAIT FOR THE "GREAT PUMPKIN" TOGETHER...
THERE IS NO "GREAT PUMPKIN"!
THERE IS TOO!!!
SCHULZ

WELL, DID THE "GREAT PUMPKIN" BRING YOU LOTS OF PRESENTS LAST NIGHT?
PERHAPS YOU DIDN'T HEAR ME, LINUS......I SAID,...
I HEARD WHAT YOU SAID!!
SCHULZ

DEAR GREAT PUMPKIN,
YOU'VE MADE A FOOL OUT OF ME FOR THE LAST TIME! I'M REALLY GOING TO TELL YOU OFF.
DON'T BURN ALL OF YOUR BRIDGES BEHIND YOU...
SIGH!
SCHULZ

YOU HAVE A TENDENCY TO TALK LOUDLY WHEN YOU GET EXCITED, DON'T YOU, CHARLIE BROWN?
WHY DO YOU SUPPOSE YOU DO THIS?
I DON'T KNOW...NO ONE HAS EVER BEEN RUDE ENOUGH TO TELL ME ABOUT IT BEFORE!
WE CRITICAL PEOPLE ARE ALWAYS BEING CRITICIZED!
SCHULZ

ALL RIGHT, NOW LET'S SEE YOU WRITE THE NUMBER SENTENCE FOR, "ONE IS LESS THAN FIVE"
1 < 5
THAT'S RIGHT!
IT IS?!
I'VE SOLVED THE NEW MATH!!
SCHULZ

TO DANCE IS TO LIVE!
FOR ME, DANCING IS AN EMOTIONAL OUTLET...
I FEEL SORRY FOR PEOPLE WHO CAN'T DANCE...
IF YOU CAN'T DANCE, YOU SHOULD AT LEAST BE ABLE TO DO A HAPPY HOP!

AN EYE PATCH? WHY IN THE WORLD SHOULD I PUT ON AN EYE PATCH?
BECAUSE I'M GOING TO TEST YOU FOR "LAZY EYE"... THIS IS ONLY A HOME TEST, BUT IT'S VERY IMPORTANT..
HERE, PUT ON THE EYE PATCH..
YO HO HO AND A BOTTLE OF RUM!
SCHULZ

I'M WEARING THIS EYE PATCH SO YOU CAN TEST ME FOR WHAT?
FOR "AMBLYOPIA EX ANOPSIA" OR WHAT IS CALLED "LAZY EYE"
"AMBLYOPIA" REFERS TO DIMNESS OF VISION, AND "EX ANOPSIA" TO THE LACK OF USE WHICH IS RESPONSIBLE FOR THE DIMNESS OF VISION
ARE YOU SURE THIS DOESN'T HAVE SOMETHING TO DO WITH THE "NEW MATH"?
OH, GOOD GRIEF!
SCHULZ

ALL RIGHT, SALLY, WE'RE READY NOW TO TEST YOU FOR "LAZY EYE"
I'M GOING TO HOLD UP THIS MODIFIED ILLITERATE "E" CHART, AND I WANT YOU TO..
ILLITERATE?! I'M NOT ILLITERATE! I'M JUST AS AS GOOD AS ANYONE! I WAS BORN IN THIS COUNTRY!
I EVEN HAVE MY OWN I.Q.! I DIDN'T COME HERE TO BE INSULTED!
SIGH
SCHULZ

WELL, I HOPE YOU'RE SATISFIED! I HAVE TO GO SEE AN OPHTHALMOLOGIST!
BUT JUST BECAUSE YOU FAILED OUR HOME EYE TEST, IT DOESN'T MEAN SOMETHING IS DEFINITELY WRONG WITH YOUR EYES...YOU'RE LUCKY YOU'RE GETTING THEM CHECKED...
I SUPPOSE SO, BUT I CAN TELL YOU ONE THING...
I'M NOT GONNA WEAR BIFOCALS!
SCHULZ

YOU **DID** HAVE A "LAZY EYE" DIDN'T YOU?
YES, MY OPHTHALMOLOGIST SAID I HAVE TO WEAR THIS PATCH FOR SIX MONTHS..
BUT JUST THINK...AFTER THAT MY EYE WILL BE ALL RIGHT...HE PUT THE PATCH ON MY GOOD EYE SO THE WEAK ONE WILL WORK HARDER
HOW DO I LOOK WITH AN EYE PATCH?
YOU LOOK FINE...YOU REALLY DO...
I FEEL LIKE AN AD FOR MEN'S SHIRTS!
SCHULZ

I SUPPOSE YOU'RE WONDERING WHY I'M WEARING THIS EYE PATCH, EH LINUS?
YOU PROBABLY HAVE AMBLYOPIA EX ANOPSIA..THE VISION IN YOUR RIGHT EYE IS DIM SO THE DOCTOR HAS PATCHED THE LEFT ONE, THUS FORCING THE RIGHT EYE TO WORK...
ACTUALLY, TREATMENT OF AMBLYOPIA IS ONE OF THE MOST REWARDING IN MEDICINE...WITHOUT MEDICATION OR SURGERY OR HOSPITALIZATION A CHILD CAN BE GIVEN EYESIGHT IN AN EYE WHICH OTHERWISE MIGHT HAVE NO SIGHT...
YOU DRIVE ME CRAZY!!
SCHULZ

ONLY 6 DAYS UNTIL BEETHOVEN'S BIRTHDAY
ELEVEN DAYS TO THE FIRST DAY OF WINTER
ONLY 12 SHOPPING DAYS UNTIL CHRISTMAS
IT'S UNUSUAL FOR ONE AGENCY TO HAVE ALL THREE ACCOUNTS!
SCHULZ

MOMS SAYS TO GET STARTED ON YOUR HOMEWORK
TELL HER I'M CONDUCTING AN EXPERIMENT TO SEE WHAT WOULD HAPPEN TO SOMEONE WHO NEVER DID HIS HOMEWORK, BUT JUST SAT AND WATCHED TV EVERY EVENING...
MOM SAYS TO GET STARTED ON THAT HOMEWORK RIGHT NOW!
I SHOULD THINK THE RESULTS OF SUCH AN EXPERIMENT COULD PROVE TO BE QUITE VALUABLE...
SCHULZ